I AM

ENCOURAGED

30 DAYS OF SELF DECLARATIONS AND AFFIRMATIONS

RESTORATION OF THE BREACH
WITHOUT BORDERS

CHARLESTOWN , NEVIS, W.I

Published By:
Restoration Of The Breach Publishing
Lou-Mot Drive Colquhoun Estate,
Charlestown, Nevis W.I.
restorativeauthor@gmail.com
Tele: (1869) 669-4386

Ebook Cover Design By: Calbert Simson
Divine.Creativevillage@Gmail.Com

Formatting and Publishing Done By:
Sherene Morrison
Publisher.20@Aol.Com

Unless otherwise stated scripture verses are quoted from
the New King James Bible.

DEDICATION

I dedicate this devotional to those who are discouraged, fearful and doubtful. I pray that as you read you will become empowered, inspired, hopeful, determined and encouraged.

ENDORSEMENTS

Hillary Dunkley-Campbell has written a life-long impactful devotional that brings healing within and builds one's confidence in God. You need to read this Devotional! It impacted me greatly. It is a must have!

Reverend Musa Laing
Pastor,
Victory Family Center
Kingston, Jamaica

It can be a challenge to maintain a daily devotion in the midst of the hustle and bustle of daily life or find daily affirmation when facing negativity. But having an affirmation reset can be therapeutic and spiritually transformative. Transformative is what this devotional represents - a 30-day affirmation reset; 30 days of daily Bible-based, impactful declarations. These declarations are not just positive thinking and good words, they are God-words, words acknowledging that the courage comes from God; in bible terms, the joy of the Lord is my strength! In everyday language, when courage comes from the entreating of another, we call it encouragement. Sometimes we have to stand beside ourselves and encourage our own selves. Delve in, I have, and *I am Encouraged!!*

Bishop Ricardo O. Henry
Land O'Lakes Church of God
Florida
USA

ACKNOWLEDGEMENTS

I must acknowledge and give thanks to God the giver of the Holy Spirit that inspired and encouraged me to write this devotional. Had it not been for the help of the Holy Spirit this devotional would not have been written. He is my indwelling cheerleader that continually cheers me on.

Additionally, special love and appreciation to my wonderful husband Trevor Campbell, for giving me the time, space, and continued support to do the work of God. I thank the Lord for you. My gifted and beautiful children Tyrese, Tianna and Dwayne Campbell, I love and appreciate you all.

Special thank you and appreciation to my Mentor and my friend Rev. Leostone Morrison; you refuse to allow me to settle at the place of mediocrity and complacency, and is always pushing me to strive to the next level in becoming my "Better Me"

Thank you to Reverend Musa Laing, Pastor of Victory Family Centre. You have been a constant source of encouragement through your teaching and preaching of the undiluted word of God to me. I admire your passion, compassion, commitment and boldness in doing the work of God. God Bless you Sir.

Thanks and appreciation to my best friend Elsa Lawrence, my spiritual mother Lillet Wynter, my dear friend, prayer partner and big sister Donna Satahoo. Also, thanks to my spiritual sisters, Sherene Morrison, Stacy Ann "Resurrected Garvey", Kristina 'Moya" Thomas, Chaneika Laing and Shamanisha Wilmot. I thank you all for your prayers, words of encouragement and continuous support in all I do. I thank the Lord for you all.

FOREWORD

Mrs. Hillary Dunkley-Campbell is a valuable gift to the Body of Christ. I believe everyone who is pursuing greatness needs a "Hillary". She is that friend who will encourage you to maximize every possibility afforded to you. Since the day I met her, she has not ceased in encouraging me. This, she does sometimes, with great resistance. We are a part of the Next Level Let's Climb Bible Study WhatsApp Group where she is a weekly teacher. Her gift of encouraging cannot be hidden. *"I Am Encouraged"* was not written because Mrs. Hillary Dunkley-Campbell was bored and needed to occupy her time. Rather, it was written by divine instruction for assistance to those who are losing hope. What I love about this book is, the first person to be encouraged by it was the author. Her greatest challenge in encouraging was not from others but from herself. She is her greatest critic, which sometimes works against her. However, when she received this assignment from the Lord, like Moses, she had her excuses. She said, "I am not a writer nor am I eloquent enough". She also compared herself to a few persons who she thought would be better at completing the assignment. Despite her informal petitions to God, He was not disturbed. The assignment remained with her. She had to live this 30 Day Devotional. I am confident that what *"I Am Encouraged"* did for the author, it will do for you too. She is encouraged to be an Encourager.

Rev. Leostone Morrison
Author
Mind Renewal, Biblical Secrets To A Better You
&
Marriage Reconstruction

Introduction

Merriam-Webster dictionary defines encourage as 'to inspire with courage, spirit or hope". There is a well-known song by Donald Lawrence and the Tri-City Singers called "Encourage Yourself". The lyrics reads as follows: "Sometimes you have to encourage yourself, sometimes you have to speak victory during the test, and no matter how you feel, speak the word and you will be healed. Speak over yourself, encourage yourself in the Lord." "I am Encouraged" is in harmony with the lyrics to this song. There will be times when you must encourage yourself in the Lord. Your family and friends may not be around to help you to do so in times when you need encouragement. You live in a broken world, where you will experience discouragement, stress, disappointments, losses, rejection, brokenness, pain and suffering. There is no escaping it. The word of God – The Bible is where you can go to find words of encouragement for every situation you maybe confronting. Proverbs 30:5 tell you " Every word of God is pure; He is a shield to those who put their trust in Him" I am Encouraged" is 30 days of self-declarations and affirmations written by the inspiration of the Holy Spirit through the word of God to help you encourage yourself in the Lord.

How to use this book

The daily devotionals are written on a first-person narrative where the reader can insert their name in the blank spaces provided. This allows the reader to truly personalize and affirm the words that they are reading to encourage themselves in the Lord. Each day has a reflection page where the readers can journal how they are encouraged.

TABLE OF CONTENTS

Day 1
Dear Me

Proverbs 23:7

For as he thinks in his heart, so is he.
"Eat and drink!" he says to you,
but his heart is not with you.

Dear_____,

It's time for me go to the next level and become who the Lord has ordained me to be, a handsome/beautiful, powerful, distinguished, multi-talented, man/woman of God. It's time for me to stop allowing doubt and fear to prevent me from becoming a better me. I am destined for greatness. Therefore, I refuse to settle for less. My mediocre way of thinking has come to an end. The Lord has blessed me with a great mind, and it is now time for me to use it. My mind is being renewed to believe that I can do all things through Christ that gives me strength. The Holy Spirit has granted me great wisdom, ability and expertise to do the work of the Lord. I concur with the songwriter who said, "I am no longer a slave to fear". If I can think it, I can do it! Expectancy and expansion have become my new norm. God has aligned me with men and women of God to help me on my journey to becoming a better me. I shall learn from them, appreciate them and pray for them. I believe and pursue the promises of God. I am determined to work towards it wholeheartedly with confidence in God that I shall achieve it. There is no failure in me because God is faithful and lives in me! I've got this! God's got me! The "Better Me" awaits me!

Yours truly,

_____

Prayer

Lord you have the copyright to my life to do with me as you please. I may not agree with your choices at times, but by your grace and mercy I will fall into alignment with your will in Jesus' name. Amen.

Declaration

I am too valuable to God to be thinking so low of myself.

Reflection

I am encouraged to:

_____

_____

_____

_____

_____

_____

Day 2
Note to Self

Psalm 139:13-14

For You formed my inward parts;
You covered me in my mother's
womb. I will praise You, for I am
fearfully and wonderfully made;
Marvelous are Your works,
And that my soul knows very well.

I can do all things through Christ who gives me strength. I am a God pleaser, not a man pleaser. I will stop comparing myself to others. God made me unique and that's okay. Why am I trying so hard to fit in? It's okay to be different, to stand out, to be uncommon. I am fearfully and wonderfully made by God. "I cannot" is no longer a part of my vocabulary. "I can", and "I will" is my new language and I will speak it with confidence. I have the mind of Christ;

therefore, I decree and declare that I have perfect knowledge and understanding of every situation with the help of the Holy Spirit. God has His hands upon me therefore; I will no longer allow insecurities to paralyze me from becoming who God has ordained me to be. I will stop fluctuating between confidence and doubt. I purpose to believe in the God that lives within me. I will stop focusing on the weaknesses of my shortcomings and turn them into my strengths. I am like the tree planted by the river that is bearing fruit in its season. The favor of God is upon my life. Therefore, in everything I do I shall prosper. The Lord delights in blessing me and I take great honor in receiving His blessings upon my life. It's now up to me to begin to pursue, conquer and win in Jesus' name and just do it!

Prayer

Lord, grant me understanding of who I am in you. Teach me to love me as how you love me.

Amen.

Declaration

I will praise you Lord, for I am fearfully and wonderfully made by you. Mighty are the works of your hand upon my life.

Reflection

I am encouraged to:

_____

_____

_____

_____

_____

_____

Day 3
Don't be Scared, I Can Do This!

2 Timothy 1:7

For God has not given us a spirit of
fear, but of power and of love and of
a sound mind.

*F*ear is not of God. For God has not given me a spirit of fear, but of power, of love and of a sound mind. I have the power within me to conquer fear. The Lord has promised me that if I seek Him, He will answer me and deliver me from all my fears (Psalms 34:4). Therefore, I will not allow fear to belittle me and make me feel inferior. No longer will I listen to the lies that I am incompetent, not worthy or smart enough. Fear, you are being silenced with the word of God that tells me, even though I walk through the valley of the shadow of death, I will fear no evil, for the Lord is with me; his rod and staff, they comfort me (Psalms 23:4). Fear, your time in my life has come to an end. You are now evicted and no longer welcome here.

I can, and I will do this! Purpose and destiny are calling me, and I will not allow you fear to stop me from answering them. If the All-knowing God placed it in my spirit, in my mind and in my heart, He will equip me with the tools to accomplish it. A man's gift makes room for him (Proverbs 18:16), which means God has positioned everything in place for me to fulfill what He is calling me to do. Fear, you have nothing on me because the Lord is my light and my salvation; whom shall I fear? The Lord is the stronghold of my life; of whom shall I be afraid? Fear, you will not name me, as my name is Victory_____.

Prayer

Heavenly Father, I rebuke and cast out the spirit of fear. You have been operating illegally and it's time for you to go in Jesus' name. Amen.

Declaration

The Spirit of God lives in me. Therefore, I shall not fear.

Reflection

I am encouraged to:

_____

_____

_____

_____

_____

_____

Day 4
Only Me Can Stop Me

Philippians 1:6

Being confident of this very thing,
that He who has begun a good work
in you will complete it until the day
of Jesus Christ.

Only me can stop me from my purpose. As of today, I am putting a stop order on procrastination, doubt, fear, delay, defeat, hopelessness and laziness. The time is now for me to begin operating in my new normalcy of greatness, excellence and expectation. Strength and honor are my clothing, and I will wear them with grace and confidence in God. I will stop telling myself that "I will fail" but say I shall win! God saw that there was a need and He created me to fulfill it. Therefore, I will stop delaying and allow the spirit of God to work within me to complete the great work that He has begun in me. I am a winner; I was born to win! I am who God says I am - highly favored among men! My faith in God has been activated to a higher level where doubt and fear do not reside.

The Lord promised to give me a future filled with hope, his faithfulness and love. I am not too old or too young for this. God used Moses when he was at his mature age to lead the Israelites to freedom from the Egyptians, and he used Jeremiah, a young man to become a prophet over the nations. No more excuses. Let's go. Yes, me! Get up! It's time to move forward and do this, my destiny and nations await me.

Prayer

Dear God, thank you Lord for choosing me, your humble servant, to do your work. I cannot do this without you Lord. I am solely relying on you to help me do this. I am confident that you will not disappoint me nor forsake me. Amen.

Declaration

I shall complete the good work that God has begun in me until the day of Jesus Christ.

Reflection

I am encouraged to:

_____

_____

_____

_____

_____

_____

Day 5
God is My Strength

Psalm 46:1

God is our refuge and strength, a very
present help in trouble.

*M*y strength comes from the Lord. He gives me the fortitude and courage to run through troops and leap over walls. In the book of Nehemiah 2:10 Sanballat and Tobiah tried to hinder the rebuilding of the wall of Jerusalem by trying to stop, intimidate and discourage Nehemiah into quitting or running away from his assignment. Like Nehemiah, I will not allow anyone to force me into aborting my assignment. God is my anchor that holds me in the midst of the storm. Though the waters may be rough and the storms of life are raging, I will not lose hope. Jesus is my lifeguard and the captain of my ship. I will take courage in Him and keep my eyes focused on Him. I won't get distracted by life's disappointments, setbacks, heartaches and pain. God needs me to be bold, strong, and very courageous. My strength and faith in Him will foster a more intimate relationship with Him. I must be strong in the Lord and in the power of His might. I will continue to wear the whole armor of God and stand against the wiles of the enemy. My flesh and my heart may fail, but God is the strength of my heart and my portion forever (Psalm 73:26). God has given me the power over all the powers of the enemy. My weakness is made strong in Him who fuels my determination to succeed. He is the fire that ignites my will to fight and to never submit to defeat or failure. God is my strength; on him I can depend.

Prayer

Heavenly Father, thank You for being my strength, my shield, and my strong tower in the time of the storm and when I am weak; You reassure me daily through your words of your strength and protection of me. I am forever grateful and thankful to you for your love for me.

Amen.

Declaration

The Lord is my Strength; I will remain confident in him.

Reflection

I am encouraged to:

_____

_____

_____

_____

_____

_____

Day 6
Endure the Process

Ecclesiastes 9:11

I returned and saw under the sun that
the race is not to the swift, Nor the
battle to the strong,
Nor bread to the wise, Nor riches to
men of understanding,
Nor favor to men of skill;
But time and chance happen to them
all.

I must endure the process. Like a rare and precious diamond in the rough, I must go through a rigorous process that will mold and shape me into a sparkling, beautiful, masterpiece of God. The process was not meant to break me, but rather to teach me perseverance, endurance and total reliance on God. Hebrews 12: 1 reminds me to lay aside every weight, and the sin which so easily ensnares *me*, I will run with

21

endurance the race that is set before me. I will not allow myself to despise the process. Instead, I will embrace it and use it as training to run the race that is set before me.

 The process is a part of God's plan to take me to my divine purpose. The process will require me to change my thinking, my attitude and adopt the ways of God to function at the level He wants me to. He is the creator of the process; He knows my limitations and will not give me more than I can bear. He is holding my hand and directing me through the process. I am created anew in Christ Jesus, so I can do the good things He has planned for me long ago. (Ephesians 2:10). I am positioning myself to fulfill my purpose which equals success in God. The promises of God will never fail me with his grace I will endure till the end to reap the rewards.

Prayer

Oh Lord, help me to understand that the process is not meant to break me. I should embrace it and use it as a tool to push me into my divine purpose.

Amen.

Declaration

I shall endure the process and be victorious in Jesus' name.

Reflection

I am encouraged to:

_____

_____

_____

_____

_____

_____

Day 7
My Help Comes from God

Psalm 121:1-2

I will lift up my eyes to the hills —
from whence comes my help?
My help comes from the Lord, Who
made heaven and earth.

God, I need your help today. I cannot do this on my own. You are my refuge and strength, a very present help in my time of trouble. When the Lord heard the Israelites cry for help in Exodus 3: 9 as they were being enslaved by the Egyptians, He sent Moses to rescue them. God, you are my Moses today. Lord, I need you; please hasten to my rescue. Help me to trust in you God with all my heart. I confess that there are days when I feel strong, but there are days when I feel weak. Today,

Lord I need your strength to pull me through. The odds are stacked against me to fail, but I will not despair. Lord, I reject the pull to attempt this on my own. The battle is not mine; it belongs to You. You are my support, my stronghold, my shield, my place of refuge. Therefore, I am confident that defeat is not my portion. God your faithfulness to me is incomparable and empowers me to never give up, but to fight. You, Lord, arm me with strength for battle and make my way perfect. In you I will not retreat. I will fight. I am a solider in the army of God. I believe that the battle has been fixed for me to win. My victory is guaranteed in you Lord.

Prayer

Thank you Lord for inclining your ears to my prayer; I know without a doubt that help is already here. Help me to be patient and remain steadfast in you.

Amen.

Declaration

God is my help. I will not be shaken; I will not be moved.

Reflection

I am encouraged to:

_____

_____

_____

_____

_____

_____

Day 8
Pray without Ceasing

1 Thessalonians 5:16-18

Rejoice always, pray without ceasing,
in everything give thanks; for this is
the will of God in Christ Jesus for you.

I will never give up on prayer. I will pray and pray, and then pray some more. God wants me to pray without ceasing. He wants me to call on Him; He will answer and show me great and mighty things. Jesus encourages me to always pray and not lose heart. Prayer is the key that unlocks the heavenly doors and grants me access to the throne of grace. This is God's promise: whatever I ask in prayer according to His will with faith, I will receive it. I will not be concerned about how to pray. I will pray with my praise and worship; I will pray with my tears, and my words. God has me covered! My loving and eternal Father gave me a prayer partner that lives within me, the Holy Spirit, who searches my heart and knows the mind of the spirit that intercedes, guides, inspires and strengthens me in prayer. It is not wise of me to allow Satan to stop me from praying. Satan knows how to affect my prayers and will do everything within his power to stop me from praying. Through Christ I have the power and the authority over him and his demons. Therefore, I must function as such by the leading of the Holy Spirit.

I am reminded not to worry about anything, instead, pray about everything: to tell God what I need and thank Him for all He has done. I am rejoicing and giving God thanks for hearing and answering my prayers in Jesus name.

Prayer

Lord, grant me the grace to pray and stir up the passion in me for prayer. Thank you, Lord, for inclining your ears to my prayer.

Amen.

Declaration

My prayers shall not be hindered in Jesus Name.

Reflection

I am encouraged to:

_____

_____

_____

_____

_____

_____

Day 9
My Promise Name from God

1 Peter 2:9

But you are a chosen generation, a
royal priesthood, a holy nation, His
own special people, that you may
proclaim the praises of Him who
called you out of darkness into His
marvelous light

*G*od called Gideon a mighty Man of Valor: that was his promise name. My promise name is son/daughter of the most high God. I am the light in the darkness of this world. I am an ambassador for Christ. I will not allow the enemy to change my name or my identity. My past sin is not my name or who I am in Christ today. I am a Child of God. I am a new creation. The old me has passed away; behold, the new me is born. I am royalty. My daddy is the King of Kings and the Lord of Lords. I am co-heir with Christ. The Lord has chosen me for Himself as His special treasure.

Just like Gideon, I thought I wasn't good enough. I didn't measure up. I wasn't important enough to do what God is calling me to do. But God looked beyond my insecurities, flaws, doubts, fears and what the world was calling me, and God called me by my name, "A mighty man/woman of Valor!" My promise name identifies me with my assignment given by God. He calls me Overcomer, Conqueror, Chosen, Blessed, Favored, Forgiven and Victor.

According to John 15:15, Jesus also calls me friend. Jesus is the friend that will always be there to support, encourage and love me unconditionally. Being called a friend of God will come with attacks from my adversaries. But my relationship with Jesus assures me that I shall be victorious, and my adversaries shall be defeated. Therefore, today I celebrate my promise name; I am a friend of God.

Prayer

Heavenly Father, I thank you for my promise name. Help me Lord to not believe the lies of the enemy when he calls me by names that you have not given me. Let me answer to no other name than those you have called me in Jesus' name.

Amen.

Declaration

I am who God says I am.

Reflection

I am encouraged to:

_____

_____

_____

_____

_____

_____

Day 10
The Promises of God Still Stands

2 Corinthians 1:20

For all the promises of God in
Him are Yes, and in Him Amen, to
the glory of God through us.

_____ the promises of God still stands! If God says it, that settles it! My God is a God of character and integrity: He honors His word above His name. I believe in the integrity and the ability of God to deliver on His promises; God specializes in doing the impossible. His word says, "The things which are impossible with men are possible with God" (Luke 18:27). God promised Gideon in Judges 6:16 "Surely I will be with you, and you shall defeat the Midianites as one man." The promise given was in twofold, the reassurance of God's presence and guaranteed victory over the enemy through the power of God. I am grateful to God that I have the same promises today. As a child of God, I have a right to claim the promises of God. I reject the enemy's lies that tell me otherwise.

The journey of receiving the promises of God will come with challenges but God is faithful. My human intellect is limited in understanding the process associated with the fulfillment of the promises of God. His faithfulness towards me fuels my confidence and faith in Him Therefore; I must take God at His word and trust Him to deliver on His promises to me. His record testifies to Him being a way maker, a miracle worker. He is not like us human therefore He is incapable of not fulfilling on His promises. God has never broken a promise: they are Yes and Amen in Christ (2 Corinthians 1:20).

Prayer

Thank you Lord, for being a promise keeper; Your promises are secured, signed, sealed and delivered. Help me to stand on your promises.

Amen.

Declaration

I will stand firm on the promises of God and I shall not be moved.

Reflection

I am encouraged to:

_____

_____

_____

_____

_____

_____

Day 11
Push, Press, Fight

Isaiah 35:4

Say to those who are fearful-hearted,
"Be strong, do not fear!
Behold, your God will
come with vengeance,
With the recompense of God;
He will come and save you.

Why should I not push, press and fight? O ye have ye little faith? God has granted me the power and the authority to rebuke the winds and calm the storms in my life. I will stop allowing the storms of life to rob me of my peace that the Lord has given me. The Lord has given me perfect peace to sleep and ride out my storm. Why am I distressed, when I know that God will not allow me to perish? I will not drown in the seas of sorrows and despair. Rise up oh my soul in the name of Jesus and take my rightful place as a child of God. This is not the time for self-pity.

The storm was meant to strengthen me, empower me and build my faith in God. Now is the time for me to elevate my faith to a higher dimension. My faith will fuel me to fight with confidence knowing that I have already won. Failure and defeat is not an option. The Lord created me for such a time as this. I have come too far: I will not back down now and settle for less than God's best. I will Push, Press and Fight! This is my winning season.

The Lord will make a way for me. The Lord will fight for me and vindicate me. I will not allow my heart to be troubled. Rather, I trust and believe that God will carry me. God is with me in the storm: He promised never to leave me nor forsake me. God keeps His promises. I will have no fear and remain resilient and steadfast in God; He will see me through. I am Victorious in the name of Jesus.

Prayer

Father God, though the storms of life are raging I will not fear. I am holding on to Your hands Lord and riding out my storm in Jesus' name.

Amen.

Declaration

The storms of life will not overtake me. I will remain steadfast in God.

Reflection

I am encouraged to:

_____

_____

_____

_____

_____

_____

Day 12
Why Does This Seem So Hard?

2 Chronicles 20:15

And he said, "Listen, all you of Judah and you inhabitants of Jerusalem, and you, King Jehoshaphat! Thus says the Lord to you: 'Do not be afraid nor dismayed because of this great multitude, for the battle is not yours, but God's.

It seems hard because I allow my mind to tell me that it's hard. It's now time for me to stop allowing my mind to take me to that mediocre level of thinking. Like David who slayed the giant Goliath, who taunted the Israelites for 40 days (1 Samuel 17), every Goliath that I have created in my mind, to discourage and defeat me, must be destroyed. God has given me the anointing and the power of the Holy Spirit, to

47

slay every Goliath in my mind and elevate me to a higher level of thinking. Therefore, my mind is a reservoir of God's wisdom, might, grace and goodness.

What is my mind telling me to be? If I can conceive it, I can attain it. My mind will only go where I allow it to travel. As a man thinketh so is he. Lao Tzu writes "Watch your thoughts, they become your words; watch your words, they become your actions; watch your actions, they become your habits; watch your habits, they become your character; watch your character, it becomes your destiny."

What I'm facing maybe difficult to accomplish. However, I must adopt the same mindset as David did when he faced Goliath "You come to me with a sword, with a spear, and with a javelin. But I come to you in the name of the Lord of hosts, the God of the armies of Israel, whom you have defied…This day the Lord will deliver you into my hand" (1 Samuel 17:45-46). The greatest of victory comes out of the most intense wars. The magnitude of my fight will encourage me to push harder and not surrender to defeat.

Prayer

Lord, grant me the grace and courage to confront and defeat every Goliath I am facing in my life in Jesus' name.

Amen.

Declaration

The battle is not mine: it's the Lord's. Therefore, I shall be victorious in Jesus' name.

Reflection

I am encouraged to:

_____

_____

_____

_____

_____

Day 13
Wounded but Not Out

Psalm 147:3

He heals the brokenhearted
And binds up their wounds.

I may be battered and bruised but I am still here. God didn't allow the enemy to defeat me. Although the wounds that I sustained were meant to kill me, God used them to strengthen me; I can wear my scars as medals of honor and reminders of God's keeping power. I will not be discouraged by my scars but wear them with pride, knowing that God sustained me through this battle. I am not the same person I was before the war. The Lord shall mend my broken heart and heal my wounds.

"And we know that all things work together for good to them that love God, to them who are the called according to his purpose" (Romans 8:28). God causes everything to work together for my good. He gives the hardest battle to the strongest solider. I am strong, bold and courageous! I am celebrating because I am victorious. The Lord has given me beauty for ashes. (Isaiah 61:3) I offer thanksgiving unto God: He has given me great success through Jesus Christ. It's now time to reap the rewards and benefit from the wealth of my scars. The tears that are flowing are not tears of sorrow but tears of joy. I went to war and survived. I am giving God the Glory and the praise for my victory. I didn't die but I lived to walk in my divine purpose. I was wounded but not defeated.

I am wearing my dancing shoes and doing my victory dance before the Lord. Victory today is mine! Not only today, but perpetual victory is mine. I am always winning.

Prayer

Thank you, Lord, for not allowing me to die on the battlefield; I was wounded and scared, but you granted me the victory in Christ Jesus.

Amen.

Declaration

I am a victor not a victim. I have the Victory in Jesus.

Reflection

I am encouraged to:

_____

_____

_____

_____

_____

_____

Day 14

Not Knowing What To Do

Proverbs 3:5-6

Trust in the Lord with all your heart,
And lean not on your own
understanding;
In all your ways acknowledge Him,
And He shall direct your paths.

There are times when I don't know what to do.
Not knowing what to do is not such a bad
position for me to be in. Being in this position
grants me the opportunity to seek the Lord with
the understanding that I must solely rely on Him
to give me the answers and carry me through.
God is the only wise-God: He has all the answers
to the many questions I am asking. Why Lord?
Why did this have to happen to me? Why now?

God, where are you? God is intentional about me; He knows what I can and cannot handle. God is going to only share with me what He knows I can handle. What if God told me that I'm going to die a horrible death like Jesus? How would I handle that? You see, God cannot reveal all the plans He has for me in the present time. God allows me to get a glimpse at times, to slowly unravel His plans towards me.

His word says in Jeremiah 29:11 "For I know the thoughts that I think toward you, says the Lord, thoughts of peace and not of evil, to give you a future and a hope". I must be patient and submit to Him and allow Him to have His way in my life and refrain from leaning on my own understanding (Proverbs 3:5). I may not know what to do today, but I am seeking the Lord with faith believing that He will tell me what to do.

Prayer

Lord, I am looking to You for the answers as I don't know what to do In Jesus' name.

Amen.

Declaration

The Lord is the author of my life: He is writing my story.

Reflection

I am encouraged to:

_____

_____

_____

_____

_____

_____

Day 15
Rejection

Psalm 27:10

When my father and my mother
forsake me, then the Lord will take
care of me.

*B*eing rejected will hurt me. But I will not allow the hurt to stop me from moving forward. I must work the rejection in my favor and to my advantage. Similarly, Jesus' rejection by man worked in my favor by giving me the gift of salvation and grace. My obedience to God will come with rejection. My rejection is opening doors for me to discover my strength in God. I refuse to allow rejection to make me become bitter, angry and unforgiving. It will not fester and become toxic to my soul. My mind has been renewed to not despise being rejected but to see the wealth in rejection.

The crowd chose Barabbas a robber and rejected Jesus. Divine rejection! God orchestrated my rejection: it's a part of His divine plan for my life. His rejection made me a part of a holy nation and redeemed me from sin and shame. I am now the righteousness of God in Christ Jesus. I shall not dwell at the place of rejection; it's not a place I will tarry for long. I will walk pass it with thanksgiving unto God knowing that He has "His best" awaiting me. Had I not been rejected it would not have given me the opportunity to discover my purpose. Rejection propelled me into my "Next". It has served its purpose for me to grow and acquire knowledge from it.

The greatness in me will expose me to rejection. In Genesis 37 Joseph shared his dreams of greatness and was rejected by his brothers, thrown into a pit, then sold into slavery. His rejection sent him from the pit to the palace. As in Joseph's life, the rejection that was meant for evil, God has turned it around for my good. I will rejoice in the face of rejection: it's the forerunner to my divine destiny!

Prayer

Mighty God, help me to see the wealth in being rejected in Jesus' name.

Amen.

Declaration

There is no rejection in Jesus.

Reflection

I am encouraged to:

_____

_____

_____

_____

_____

_____

Day 16
Expansion in Pain

2 Corinthians 4:16-18

Therefore, we do not lose heart. Even
though our outward man is perishing,
yet the inward man is being renewed
day by day. For our light affliction,
which is but for a moment, is working
for us a far more
exceeding and eternal weight of
glory, while we do not look at the
things which are seen, but at the
things which are not seen. For the
things which are seen are temporary,
but the things which are not
seen are eternal.

We are familiar with the account of Hagar, Sarah's maid servant in Genesis 16. Sarah gave her to Abraham to produce a son, Ishmael. Afterwards, Sarah treated Hagar badly and she ran away. But Look what the Lord told

66

her to do: "The angel of the Lord said to her, "Return to your mistress, and submit to her authority" (Genesis 16:9). The Lord told her to go back to being abused, go back and endure the pain, the hardship. But just like Hagar my pain is not wasted; there is purpose in my pain. Hagar's pain birthed this promise from God. Then the Angel of the Lord said to her, "I will multiply your descendants exceedingly, so that they shall not be counted for multitude" (Genesis 10:16).

What is my pain giving birth to? My pain is giving birth for me to produce, to increase, to expand, to excel. It's hard to comprehend at times why God would allow me to go through such pain and suffering. But I know God is with me in my pain. My pain will help me to grow spiritual muscles, give me spiritual stamina to run and endure the race that is set before me. This race is a long one and I don't know when it's going to end. I may experience, exhaustion, aches, pains, frustration, roadblocks, tough terrains, delays, fatigue. As I run in this race, I must remember that this race is fixed for me to win. The outcome is already predetermined. Just like with Eve and Hagar, there is much to be gained from my pain. Pain gave birth to life. And so it is with me the pain that I am experiencing at this present time will push me into birthing my purpose and elevate me to a place in God where I am rooted and grounded in Him. If I stay committed and obedient to my God - Victory is a MUST!

Prayer

Lord, it's difficult at times to endure the pain and I pray that you will take it away. But if you choose not at this time, please grant me the grace to endure it in Jesus' name.

Amen.

Declaration

The Lord will sustain me; I shall not be moved.

Reflection

I am encouraged to:

_____

_____

_____

_____

_____

_____

Day 17
I Am Equipped for This

Hebrews 13:21

Make you complete in every good
work to do His will, working in you
what is well pleasing in His sight,
through Jesus Christ, to
whom be glory forever and ever.
Amen.

God has equipped me for this. He knew that I would need help in fulfilling my destiny. Therefore, he gave me the Holy Spirit, my indwelling cheerleader, my GPS. He has also given me the gift of prayer to communicate with him and his book of promises – His Word. I am like a marathon runner that's in training and I must use the tools that God has given me to endure the pain of running in this race. The Psalmist writes "weeping may endure for a

71

night, but joy comes in the morning light" (Psalms 30:5) the barriers and objections I am confronting have an expiration date and I have been equipped to endure and overcome.

The opportunities given are for me to expand both spiritually and physically. This is not the time for me to abandon my assignment. I will not pause. I must pursue! Be Intentional! There is a quote that says, "Tough times don't last, only tough people do". There must be brokenness before restoration. No boxer gets a trophy without a fight. Life is a fight. I don't get to sit down and have a pity party: it's those who fight that win. I am a fighter! I will fight in the name of Jesus, with the tools that God has equipped me with to achieve my divine purpose. I will not allow the enemy to overtake me.

Prayer

Lord, you have equipped me with the tools to fight. Teach me Lord how to use them to defeat the enemy in Jesus' name. Amen.

Declaration

I am determined to win in this war. I will not be defeated.

Reflection

I am encouraged to:

_____

_____

_____

_____

_____

Day 18
How Determined Am I?

Romans 12:11-12

Not lagging in diligence, fervent in
spirit, serving the Lord; rejoicing in
hope, patient in
tribulation, continuing steadfastly in
prayer;

How determined am I? How determined am I to push pass my uncertainties, my inadequacies, the naysayers, and acquire what God is calling me to do? I am potentially Entrepreneur, PhD recipient, a Pastor, a Bishop, _____. I am who God has created me to be. I will not abort my purpose or go into premature labor. I can do all things through Christ who strengthens me! I am more than a conqueror! The greater One lives in me. My disabilities have

75

become abilities. My disadvantages are now advantages.

I am determined to follow in the steps of Jesus. He knew what His assignment was; He was determined to fulfill it. According to Luke 1:51, "Now it came to pass, when the time had come for Him to be received up, that He steadfastly set His face to go to Jerusalem". Jesus knew He would face persecution and death in Jerusalem, but He was determined to go there. He wasn't going to allow anything or anyone to stop Him. This type of determination should be characterized in my life today. God gave me a course of action, and I must move steadily toward my destination, regardless of the hazards that may confront me getting there. God's Word encourages me to "Press toward the mark for the prize of the high calling of God in Christ Jesus" (Philippians 3:14). Where there is no challenge, victory is minimized. I am determined to be intentional and to win.

Prayer

Lord, despite all the obstacles and challenges set before me, I am determined to win. Help me in my time of weakness to remain strong and steadfast in You in Jesus' name.

Amen.

Declaration

I am determined to fight, to win and keep the faith in God.

Reflection

I am encouraged to:

_____

_____

_____

_____

_____

_____

Day 19
I Am Blank

Isaiah 64:12

Will You restrain Yourself because of
these things, O Lord?
Will You hold Your peace, and afflict
us very severely?

*W*hat am I to do when I'm not hearing anything from God? Do I give up? What do I do when I don't know what to do? I'm praying and fasting but I'm still blank, waiting, crying out to God, "Where are you? Why are you not speaking to me? I need you to answer me right now!"

I am asking God, "Why are you silent?" But is God silent or is it that I'm not listening? God's silence doesn't mean that He's absent. My state of blankness is not because heaven is silent or

80

because God is upset with me. It may be because I am not yet ready to receive. Being blank is not a sign of no release, but rather a sign of delayed receipt. The teacher is always silent during the test. If I am always full then there is no need for God to pour into me, no need for me to depend on Him. Though it's challenging to do, I will rejoice and give God thanks in my period of blankness.

I must understand that God has me seated at His table with my plate set, ready to receive what heaven is serving. In the book of Daniel, it is revealed that Daniel fasted for 21 days, not for heaven to speak but for him to hear. The angel was already sent with the answer from day one. Then he said, "Don't be afraid, Daniel. Since the first day you began to pray for understanding and to humble yourself before your God, your request has been heard in heaven. I have come in answer to your prayer" (Daniel 10:12). The reality is, I don't always have it all together and there is no need for me to pretend that I do. I am blank to be filled.

Prayer

Heavenly Father, teach me to wait for you to speak in times of silence. Help me to see times of emptiness as opportunities for You to fill me and my blankness as the canvas for your work of art in and through me in Jesus' name.

Amen.

Declaration

My ears are inclined to hear from the Lord.

Reflection

I am encouraged to:

_____

_____

_____

_____

_____

_____

Day 20
Doubt

Matthew 21:21

So Jesus answered and said to them, "Assuredly, I say to you, if you have faith and do not doubt, you will not only do what was done to the fig tree, but also if you say to this mountain, 'Be removed and be cast into the sea,' it will be done.

One definition of Doubt is a feeling of uncertainty or lack of conviction. Doubt is not of God. Doubt is what the enemy uses to stop me from being who God has ordained me to be. If I allow it, doubt can shut me down, cause me to feel hopeless, discouraged, not worthy. Doubt will kill my self-confidence and lead me to question my faith in God. Doubt begins in the mind: once my mind is full of doubt, my thoughts and my actions will follow.

The Word of God says "But let him ask in faith, with no doubting, for he who doubts is like a wave of the sea driven and tossed by the wind. For let not that man suppose that he will receive anything from the Lord; he is a double-minded man, unstable in all his ways" (James 1:6-7). A mind that is full of doubt is wavering and not convinced that God's way is the best in all things. In the book of Judges, Gideon doubted God when He told him he would be a judge and leader (Judges 6). Moses doubted God when He told him to return to Egypt and lead the Israelites to freedom (Exodus 3). Both men started out as real doubters, but God showed great patience towards them in helping them to overcome their doubts. They were honest to God about their doubts, but they did not reside there. I will not reside at the place of doubt. I rebuke the spirit of doubt in the name of Jesus.

My hope and faith are in God. There is no limit to what God can do through me. I will stop wasting precious time and much needed strength by doubting. God's hands are not short in perfecting the things concerning me. God has equipped me with the tools and strength I need to do whatever He is calling me to do.

His promises are unshakable I can depend on them.

I am now feeding my faith and starving my doubts.

Prayer

Lord, help me to remove doubt from my mind and spirit in Jesus' name.

Amen.

Declaration

I will not be double-minded. I will have faith in God.

Reflection

I am encouraged to:

_____

_____

_____

_____

_____

_____

Day 21

Give It All to Jesus

Psalms 55:22

Cast your burden on the Lord,
And He shall sustain you;
He shall never permit the righteous to
be moved.

I give it all to Jesus. God wants all my problems, trials and situations. God is responsible for me. He is my Daddy, and He is not a dead-beat one. He is a great Father. He has been taking care of me before I was born. His word confirms it in Jeremiah 1:5, "I knew you before I formed you in your mother's womb. Before you were born I set you apart" I will stop worrying and stressing. I am giving all my worries and cares to God, for He cares about me.

I am not allowing the enemy to steal my joy, worship and praise unto God. God never promised that it would be easy, but He did promise that He would never leave me nor forsake me.

The stretching, the stripping and the molding I am experiencing are to build my endurance and my faith in Him. He is the potter, I am the clay. I was not built to break. I must rely on God and trust Him during the process no matter how tough it gets. The Apostle Paul writes "For I consider that the sufferings of this present time are not worthy to be compared with the glory which shall be revealed in us" (Romans 8:18). I will give it all to Jesus: He can fix it all for me. God is the master fixer. He has all the answers. Therefore, I must put my trust in Him to care for me. I surrender all to Him.

Prayer

Lord, I give it all to You. Help me not to take it back because only you can fix it for me in Jesus' name.

Amen.

Declaration

God is responsible for me. Therefore, there is no need for me to worry. God's got me.

Reflection

I am encouraged to:

_____

_____

_____

_____

_____

_____

Day 22
God Wants Me to Pray

Ephesians 6: 18

Praying always with all prayer and
supplication in the Spirit, being
watchful to this end with all
perseverance and supplication for all
the saints.

*P*rayer is having a conversation with my father, I speak He listens, He speaks I listen. Granted most of the time I may be doing the speaking and He is doing the listening. Lord, help me to listen more. Jesus gave us a very important directive that "men always ought to pray and not loose heart" (Luke 18:1). Jesus, the son of God, knew the importance of prayer. During His short time here on earth He lived a life of prayer which I as a child of God should purpose to emulate.

The devil knows that prayer is a weapon, when used effectively; it will render him powerless against me. Therefore, he will be consistent in preventing me from praying. I must not be ignorant of his strategies that are preventing me from praying: my mind being bombarded with all types of distractions, not making time to pray and being plagued with fatigue. In prayer is where I get my deliverance, my breakthroughs, my victories, and where I bare my pain to God. It's in prayer I build an intimate relationship with God. He should be the first one I choose to communicate with in all that I do. He should be my confidante, my best friend my go to person for all my needs. God is my source; He knows all things. He must be included in my plans and concerns; I don't need to run to others for help before seeking God first in prayer.

Prayer unlocks the keys to my heavenly blessings and the promises of God. I must pray without ceasing, which means me having dialogue throughout the day with my father. Philippians 4:6-7 (NLT) tells me, "Don't worry about anything; instead, pray about everything. Tell God what you need, and thank Him for all He has done. Then you will experience God's peace, which exceeds anything you can understand.

His peace will guard your hearts and minds as you live in Christ Jesus".

Prayer

Lord, grant me an appetite for prayer in Jesus' name.

Amen.

Declaration

I will continue to pray without ceasing.

Reflection

I am encouraged to:

_____

_____

_____

_____

_____

_____

Day 23
I Am Too Gifted

1 Peter 4:10

As each one has received a gift,
minister it to one another, as good
stewards of the manifold grace of
God.

There will be times when I will feel stuck, as though I cannot go forward. I am not the first and I will not be the last to be faced with this dilemma. The truth is, I wish these days would never come; but the reality is, they are bound to come. What must I do on days like these? Should I keep my foot on the brake or do I press gas and go forward? I choose to press forward knowing that my victory awaits me.

I cannot afford to stop now because I am starting some new family traditions; traditions of success, of no limits, no boundaries. I will be the difference; I will stand out and achieve great things that have never been done before in my family. I am the game changer. I am positioned to unlock unknown doors to bless me and my descendants.

Neither I, nor the keys that are given to me are ordinary. That is why I cannot take the normal or easier route which everyone is taking. I am designed to go against the norm. Upstream is where the reward I seek is waiting for me. The delight is, I am equipped for victory. Failure is not in my DNA. I am too gifted to not be victorious. *I am a Victor!*

Prayer

Lord, thank you for the gifts and talents you have given unto to me to do your work.

Amen.

Declaration

My gifts and talents from God shall make room for me.

Reflection

I am encouraged to:

_____

_____

_____

_____

_____

_____

Day 24
Greatness is Calling Me

Job 33:4

The Spirit of God has made me,
And the breath of the Almighty gives
me life.

Greatness is calling me. According to Merriam-Webster, Greatness describes someone who is "remarkable in magnitude, degree or effectiveness". Greatness refuses to be limited or controlled in any way by fear. Archbishop Duncan William describes Fear as, "a false reality that appears to be true. The enemy will enforce it to us through the mind to make it seem real". I now refuse to allow fear to paralyze me any longer; to stop me from answering the call of Greatness. Fear is not of God. The word of God says "He has not given

103

me a spirit of fear but of power and love and a sound mind" (2 Tim.1:7). Fear, you will not haunt me anymore. I rebuke you and command you in the name of Jesus Christ of Nazareth to go now to your desolate place and never return.

It is time for me to now have confidence in God and in myself that "I can do all things through Christ who strengthens me" (Phil. 4:13). God has equipped me to answer the call of Greatness. Pain, disappointments, delays and tribulation may make an appearance on the road to Greatness. However, James tells me to "count it all joy when you fall into various trials, knowing that the testing of my faith produces patience" (James 1:2). Moses' mother, Jochebed, had to put him in a basket and release him in the flow of the River Nile into his Greatness. This was painful, but the call to greatness and to fulfill purpose was greater than her pain. Her pain required a huge sacrifice.

What am I willing to sacrifice to answer the call of greatness? Greatness is calling me. I will not allow fear and life's challenges to stop me from answering the call.

Prayer

Lord, you have empowered me to answer the call of greatness. With your grace I will answer, in Jesus' name.

Amen.

Declaration

Greatness lives within me.

Reflection

I am encouraged to:

_____

_____

_____

_____

_____

_____

Day 25
I am a Kingdom Fighter

Psalm 18:2-3

The Lord is my rock and my fortress
and my deliverer;
My God, my strength, in whom I will
trust;
My shield and the horn of my
salvation, my stronghold.
I will call upon the Lord, who is
worthy to be praised;
So shall I be saved from my enemies.

I am a Kingdom Fighter. I will not go into battle without first putting on the whole armor of God. Ephesians 6:10 tell me to "Put on the whole armor of God, that you may be able to stand against the wiles of the devil". I am engaged in spiritual warfare and I will be subjected to the devil's backlash because I am no longer on his team. Therefore, I must put on every piece of the armor to resist the devil's attack and remain steadfast in God amid every battle.

Fighting in the flesh is futile. I'm not fighting against flesh and blood. This is not a physical war but a spiritual one. The fight is against principalities, against powers, against the rulers of the darkness of this age, against spiritual hosts of wickedness in the heavenly places. Each piece of the armor is important for me to wear as I stand against the attacks of Satan. I will stand therefore, having girded my waist with the belt of truth to protect me against the lies of Satan. I will put on the breastplate of righteousness to protect my heart; the helmet of salvation to cover my head and my mind from the attacks of doubt and fear. Along with the other pieces of the armor, the gospel of peace, the sword which is the word of God, and the shield of faith, I must wear all pieces of the armor daily. The armor is equipped with supernatural powers I need to defeat Satan.

I am fully equipped as a Kingdom Fighter. I have the Holy Spirit that lives within me to encourage and cheer me on; the whole armor of God that I must wear daily; the word of God and the gift of prayer. I am fully armed and equipped to win and conquer my adversary Satan and his demons.

Prayer

Lord, thank you for choosing me to be a kingdom fighter in the army of the Lord, in Jesus' name.

Amen.

Declaration

I am a kingdom fighter in the army of the Lord. I will never be defeated.

Reflection

I am encouraged to:

_____

_____

_____

_____

_____

_____

Day 26
I will be Anxious for Nothing

Psalm 94:19

In the multitude of my anxieties
within me,
Your comforts delight my soul.

I will be anxious for nothing. Why is this hard for me to do as a child of God? When I serve a God that is Omnipotent-All Powerful, Omniscience-All knowing, Omnipresence-All present. Every time I feel like worrying, I will exchange it with prayer. Lord, help me not to put my trust in people rather than You. It's easier at times for me to call and tell others my problem first than take it to God in prayer. No longer will I allow God to be a last resort. God, you will be first! David in Psalms 37: 8 tells us to fret not: it causes harm! I will stop allowing

113

Satan to bombard my mind with his lies and deception. I will not be so caught up worrying about my problems and focusing on them that I miss the solution that God has already given me. I will not miss the lessons that God is teaching me during this process.

Nothing that I go through is wasted. I will be encouraged to go through my dry and hard season by remembering that God uses these seasons to strengthen me. In Matthew 4 and Luke 4 Jesus was tempted and tired by Satan in the wilderness. He was rewarded for defeating Satan as angels immediately came and ministered unto him and he began his Ministry in the power of the Holy Spirit. Likewise, after God delivered Shadrach, Meshach, and Abed-Nego (3 Hebrew boys) from the fiery furnace the king promoted them in the province of Babylon (Daniel 3). Therefore, just like Jesus and the three Hebrew boys I will be tested and tried but if I hold fast and not give in to the devices of the enemy then I too shall be victorious. Whatever mountain I am climbing or wilderness I am going through, I must come out better than when I started. I will not waste my pain.

Prayer

Lord, help me not to be anxious but to pray and give you thanks in Jesus' name. Amen.

Declaration

I will not be anxious but pray and give thanks.

Reflection

I am encouraged to:

_____

_____

_____

_____

_____

_____

Day 27
My Faithfulness Shall be Rewarded

2 Timothy 2:13

If we are faithless,
He remains faithful;
He cannot deny Himself.

God rewards those that are faithful to Him. It was not easy at times to remain faithful to God, but I did my best with the help of the Holy Spirit to be faithful to Him. I am learning how to be humble daily and let self-decrease so Christ can increase in me. I have faced rejection, hurt and disappointments but I am determined to be submissive, obedient and remain faithful to God. His Word says that He is a rewarder of them that diligently seeks Him (Hebrews 11:6). I purpose daily to continually seek the Lord.

Many times, I have been tempted to quit and surrender to the will of the enemy, but the spirit of the Lord that lives inside of me that is giving birth to my purpose would not allow me to. The reward is too great for me to buckle under the weight of defeat. I am fighting my way to victory, to reap my reward.

Jesus faced humiliation and suffering, but He remained faithful and obedient to God. I want to be like Jesus and do the same. I will stand firm on the promises of God. My faithfulness loads me with benefits from God that empowers me to be bold, strong, courageous and victorious. God does not expect me to stand firm by my own strength. Rather in my weakness, His strength is made perfect. He desires for me to put on the Lord Jesus Christ, and not make any provision for sinful living.

Prayer

Lord, it is not easy being faithful to You. I have failed you at times, but You never gave up on me. I am resolute in being faithful to you.

Amen.

Declaration

I shall remain faithful to God and flourish in his blessings.

Reflection

I am encouraged to:

_____

_____

_____

_____

_____

_____

Day 28
Favor of God

Luke 2:52

And Jesus increased in wisdom and
stature, and in favor with God and
men.

I have found favor with the Lord. I am the
apple of God's eyes. He has granted me
amazing grace and blessings that are
immeasurable. The favor of God may have
come with a price, but it is a price I am willing to
pay. The reward of God's favor out weights the
pain I have endured.

I am flourishing in the favor of God. My cup
runs over in abundance and grandeur.   The
favor of the Lord makes me rich with riches that
no earthly currency can buy or ascertain. The
unmerited favor of God soothes my soul, calms

my fears and reminds me of His unconditional love for me. I have favor with the King like Esther (Esther 2:15), and Nehemiah (Nehemiah 2:5), to pursue and accomplish my purpose and destiny.

The favor of God has aligned me with my Destiny Helpers ordained by Him to complete the good work He has begun in me. My victory has already been established by the favor of God. The favor that God has placed over my life has purged doubt and fear from being a part of my DNA. God has turned my failure into favor, my past into my future, my sadness into joy and my pain into praise.

I will soar like the eagle that I am! The favor of God is taking me to higher heights, deeper depths, to the mountain top and even to the valley to conquer, to win, to be transformed and be renewed in Christ Jesus.

Prayer

Thank You Lord for your divine grace and favor upon my life.

Amen.

Declaration

The favor of the Lord is upon my life.

Reflection

I am encouraged to:

_____

_____

_____

_____

_____

_____

Day 29
I am Encouraged to Fight

Ephesians 6:10-20

Finally, my brethren, be strong in the
Lord and in the power of His
might. Put on the whole armor of
God that you may be able to stand
against the wiles of the devil…

I am encouraged to fight. I will never be beaten by the enemy. No defeat! No surrender! I am born to win. I will not back down from this fight. I am going in full force with the authority and power of God. I am encouraged to fight. Though I might get weary at times, I will never quit. I will never run or hide, I will stand firm and let nothing move me. I will give myself fully to the work of the Lord because my work in Him is not in vain.

When I am afraid, I will put my trust in God and rely on Him to reassure me of His love and His divine protection to keep me from harm. The weapons will form but they will not prevail against me. The lying and negative tongues will speak against me, but they shall have no effect. I am encouraged to fight, to push, to persevere, to conquer, to overcome in Jesus name.

I am encouraged to defy the odds stacked against me to lose. I am encouraged to be strong in the Lord. I am encouraged to seek the wisdom of the Lord, not rely on my intelligence. I am encouraged to take the way of escape from temptation that the Lord has provided for me. I am encouraged to fight to the very end and be victorious in Jesus. I am encouraged to be an Encourager.

Prayer

Heavenly Father, I am encouraged to be great, to fight and to win. Thanks for your grace and everlasting love towards me. Amen.

Declaration

I am encouraged to win!

Reflection

I am encouraged to:

_____

_____

_____

_____

_____

_____

Day 30
I Did It!

Deuteronomy 20:4

For the Lord your God is He who
goes with you, to fight for you against
your enemies, to save you.'

I did it! Today I am celebrating and giving God thanks because I did it! I overcame! I prevailed! I have the victory. All my hard work has paid off. I am being rewarded for walking by faith and not by sight. Despite, the delays, disappointments, trials and tribulations, I did it! I didn't allow anxiety and uncertainty to stop me. The word of God validates my victory in 1 Corinthians 15:57: "But thanks be to God! He gives us the victory through our Lord Jesus Christ".

The temptation to quit plagued me constantly. However, today I give God the Glory that He provided a way of escape, and the grace to endure and to win. Today I celebrate me. I did great! God is my divine commander; He leads me to victory when I obey Him. Like Joshua and the Israelites in Joshua 6:20, my Jericho wall has come tumbling down. I had the audacity to defy the enemy and be triumphant. I did it! I didn't fail.

I will continue to grow my faith in the Lord by reading and listening to His word, spending time in prayer and fasting. I am committed to pursuing intimacy in relationship with the Holy Spirit, my best friend. The favor of God is upon my life. Therefore, I must have perpetual victory in Jesus' name. Amen.

Prayer

Lord, I did it! I thank you for granting me the victory in Jesus' name.

Amen.

Declaration

The Lord goes with me to fight against my enemies and gives me victory in Christ Jesus.

Reflection

I am encouraged to:

_____

_____

_____

_____

_____

_____

Conclusion
I Thank you Lord

Psalm 118: 1

Oh, give thanks to the Lord, for He is
good!
For His mercy endures forever

I thank You Lord for being an Awesome God.
I thank You Lord for strength. I thank You
Lord for the courage to fight. I thank You Lord
that You are always with me and there is no
need for me to be fearful or full of doubt. I thank
You Lord that when I am overwhelmed and
discouraged You are always there to encourage
me, to push me, to empower me. I thank You
Lord for giving me the confidence to trust and
believe in You. I thank You Lord for not
allowing my enemies to triumph over me. I
thank You Lord for your joy and your peace. I

134

thank You Lord for your unconditional love. I thank you Lord that nothing can separate me from your love. I thank you Lord, that even when I am faithless You are always faithful. I thank You Lord for being my provider and supplying all my needs. I thank You Lord for your shield of protection around my life and the lives of my friends and family. I thank You Lord for not leaving me nor forsaking me. I thank You Lord that you are my ever-present help in my time of trouble. I thank you Lord that my sins are forgiven and I am washed in your blood. I thank You Lord for not giving up on me and for choosing me to be your son/daughter, your friend. I thank You Lord, for being my best friend, my confidante. I thank you Lord for the anointing and the spiritual gifts You have given me. I thank You Lord for my indwelling helper the Holy Spirit. I thank You Lord for the gift of prayer. I thank You Lord that I am encouraged!

Thank You, Lord, for hearing and answering my prayers in Jesus name. Amen.

About the Author

Hillary Dunkley-Campbell is an ambassador for Christ. She is very passionate about prayer, doing the work of God and truly loves to encourage and empower others. She is currently pursuing her bachelor's degree in Business Administration at Tyndale University in Toronto, Canada. She is the wife to Trevor Campbell and the mother to three children, Tyrese Campbell, Tianna Campbell, and Dwayne Campbell. "I am Encouraged" is her first of many books.

Made in the USA
Monee, IL
22 January 2024

51689062R00085